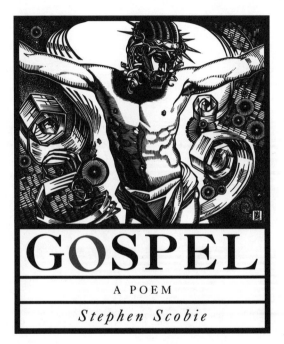

GOSPEL

A POEM

Stephen Scobie

Red Deer College Press

The Publishers
Red Deer College Press
56 Avenue & 32 Street Box 5005
Red Deer Alberta Canada T4N 5H5

Cover art by Douglas B. Jones
Design by Dennis Johnson
Printed and bound in Canada by Parkland
ColourPress Ltd. for Red Deer College Press

Financial support provided by the Alberta
Foundation for the Arts, a beneficiary of the
Lottery Fund of the Government of Alberta,
and by the Canada Council, the Department
of Communications and Red Deer College

Canadian Cataloguing in Publication Data
Scobie, Stephen, 1943 –
Gospel
(Writing West)
Poems.
ISBN 0-88995-116-0
1. Jesus Christ – Poetry. I. Title. II. Series
PS8587.C6G6 1994 C811'.54 C93-091918-1
PR9199.3.S36G6 1994

In the beginning
was the Word, and the Word
was made flesh

> — wonder of flesh that
> stutters and sings
> all measures of delight
> and pain —

and the Word is become
divisible, I am
that word that is spoken

and speaks now to you

> — word among worlds
> inheritance of Babel:
> beloved
> this is the world, we're
> in it together —

I am the word and Word:
I am that marriage, I
am the bridegroom and
I am the bride

> — I am the carpenter, I
> am the carpenter's son

4| You are going to have to take me
at my word. In writing.
Let us make this contract
between us. I who am The Word
agree to cage myself in words:
I will write for you
and with you. You undertake
to read, as if that were a simple
act of creation. Recall:
"Let there be light," my
father once said, and there was
the word "light."
Also, the word "dark."
Reader, I am prepared
to enter this darkness with you
and I'm counting on you
to bring me
again to the light
of my father's grace.

Losing memory. The first fall.
It is strange to be watching this
"from the outside." There is no
outside-the-text, for the text is
God. Is me, the Word made Flesh,
falling. As, now, I commit myself
to an alien form (the human body,
writing), I am both I and "he" — or
He. The living Christ, Immanuel.
I remember I forgot: I had to.
Fed by blood in the rhythmic womb
I danced in the chora, wordless.
Logos infans. And yet I forgot
nothing: I knew the necessity
of the whole grand scheme: atonement,
incarnation. I willed myself
towards forgetting: I desired
some years of not desiring, some years
of simple time. Perhaps as a carpenter's
son. But the angels would not let me,
interfering. And at my first cry,
a hundred newborn died. That
I can never forget. I do not come
to bring peace, but the sword.
Already the tree was planted, growing
the wood a carpenter would shape
into a cross. I knew
and did not know that, lying
in Mary's arms, in the manger,
forgetting. Observing myself forget.
Losing memory. Becoming human.

6 | I am become Flesh.
The oxen proclaim it
in whose stable I lie
using their straw.
The sheep of the fields
whose wool will warm me
are herded into the news
the angels announce
to their puzzled keepers.
The donkey with bowed head
pays tribute to my birth.
Here in the stable
(outcast from the inn, ignored
by the tax-paying customers)
I lie in glory.
The light of my father's grace
shines round me. My mother
is bending towards me. A star
shines in the cold
unmeasuring heaven. Tonight
is history's hinge, for
I am born.
The world has become at last
the home of God.
Incarnate, I cry for food.
Immanuel, I reach for milk.

I learned to use the word "home" —
to think of it as Nazareth,
as a named place in history:

to think of it as stone,
as muddy streets and plastered walls;
to think of it as the carpenter's shop
and the kitchen fire, my
father's and my
mother's house: home

as the place where I was
at home:

and all that abstract heaven

(which now I could only envision
in human terms, of gold
and chrysoprase,
with gates of pearl
and eternal
ghostlike angels)

as a place I had once
in a dream passed through,
as temporary
as smoke or toothache

the morning after

the night before

I loved to see wood
working: not what we did to it,
Joseph and I, with plane and hammer,
but the wood itself
taking shape, declaring a purpose,
writing itself in the lines of its grain
as "table," "chair," the human
form it had chosen (like me)
to become. I loved the scent
of oil and turpentine, the cedar chips
that clung to the dusty hair
of Joseph's forearm, or stuck
in the sweat of his brow
where he wiped his hand. My father
as I remember him:
in the hour at evening, downing tools
and reaching his hand towards me
awkwardly, as if
he would have liked to muss my hair
but didn't know how, not being
certain, ever, who I was.
And my (equally) uncertain grin,
not yet being sure enough
to tell him.
　　　　　Father, forgive me —
I didn't know what I was doing.
I didn't see the shape
the wood was taking. I still
loved the sound the hammer made
driving in nails.

Slip of the wrist, as Joseph
works with the chisel, gashes
deep into the palm of his hand
a red hole, opened on flesh
as I've never seen it before:
inside the body, a secret song.

He's gripping it tight, looking round
for something to wrap as a bandage:
meanwhile I lift his hand, I
reach my finger into the hole —
doubting. Believing.

And as I take my finger away
the wound closes after it,
heals. As if it's never been.

We don't know what to say about this,
for months we never mention it.
Not even to Mary. It becomes
another mystery between us,
father and son.

Father, why have you made me
like this? My question
was not embarrassed, it was only
curiosity: the body I knew
no longer so comfortably known,
the movement in my groin
not under my control. I wanted
a simple answer. But for Joseph,
Joseph of all men,
there was none. If he had said:
That is how men lie with women,
might I not have replied:
Do you lie so with Mary?
And if he had said:
That is how men and women
make children, might I not have asked:
Was I made so?
And how could he have answered me?
Father,
I said to him, Father —
why have you made me like this?

He hammered a board and pretended
not to have heard me. Years went by
until I understood
I need only have looked in his eyes
and watched him watching Mary
smooth out their bed as the evening darkness
gathered round. Meanwhile

I buried the question, I
lived with the answer.

There is this stillness, always, in my mother's eyes
in which I can sink myself, as if in the depth of heaven,
that calls me from the noise and sawdust of the shop
into the room of silence where she lives in prayer.

(She had not told me yet about the angel
or how, since then, the light and silence filled her,
made every dawn Annunciation, every night
the falling of vast feathered wings.)

But when I try to sleep, she sits beside me
smiling, her own eyes closed to encourage mine,
and then I ask her, mother, guess, my eyes
are they still open? open, mother? till they close

and in the grace of darkness both our dreams are one.

All through my childhood, the Roman
soldiers of occupation. Standing
in the door of the carpenter's shop, I'd see
the dusty gleam of helmets passing
or hear the clanking of their armour, the creak
of leather trappings. You never saw them
alone, or afraid, as they must have been —
stranded so far from home, surrounded
by a Name of God no one would even speak.
We watched with sullen suspicion: patrols
through the markets by day, or by night
the sudden raid on a zealot's house. Sometimes
they commandeered our aid, repairs to a cart
or a shaft for a spear: and Joseph
did what he had to, but still did it well
with a craftsman's pride. I began to learn
a few words of their language: *pater*,
deus, religio, mors. All through my childhood
they marched and countermarched, in centuries
across the gardens of our promised land.

You might say it was only
a slip of the tongue, a mistake:
but no,
it was not so simple.

Jerusalem, my first time there,
the holy precincts of the Temple.
I hadn't meant to stay so long
but it was such fun
debating with the scribes the scriptures
I loved like the bones
of my growing body. Like a child
I forgot the time —

and when they came looking, worried
with the fear of human parents,
I was surprised. I didn't feel guilty.
"It's all right," I said, "don't you know
I must attend to my father's business?"

It just slipped out, immediately
I wanted it back. Joseph was stunned,
the hurt like a hammer all over his face,
he turned away, stepped back, looked anywhere
for somewhere to go. And all my heart
went aching after him, and followed him

another twenty years.

Now in my thirtieth year
I offer this prayer
of thanks to my father

for the gift of the five human senses

for the taste of goat's cheese
    pungent as autumn in my mouth
    and circled with red wine

for the song the wind makes, silver
    in the chorus of the olive leaves
    blowing against each other

for the smell of wood shavings
    still redolent with sap
    flaked on the carpenter's floor

for the colours of sunrise, amber
    that bursts into blue
    over the eastern hills of Galilee

for the touch of my mother's hand
    cool, in the hours I lay sick,
    against the fever of my brow

the gift of the five human senses
multiplied by all my human years

Debate the death of God, the death
of the Father:
            my father
is Joseph the carpenter, workman of Nazareth,
and he, old in his human years,
is dying.
          I watch this death and wait
for the release it brings, baptismal blessing,
to his sweet soul.
              To Mary too, my mother,
set free
        into the blue serenity of heaven.
She blesses me. We buried him
with his workman's tools beside him,
hammer and plane, in the honest earth.
I carved his name, then set
my chisel aside. It had become the time —

— it had become John's time. My cousin,
twice he baptised me:

            in the waters of Jordan
            with his words
            with the holy dove
            that hovered in air:

                and in his blood
                with his severed head
                on the silver plate
                at Herod's table.

16| Debate how God still dies
a million times each day

in the carpenter's shop
in the tyrant's court
in the mother's kiss
in the holy, speaking, unspeakable dove.

Forty days and
forty nights
in the harsh land of Hebron
on the mountains
in the dry places of desert
a trickle of water
only, for thirst
a handful of food
hallucination
the shaman's dreams
initiation

Satan as a scorpion
(he comes in many guises):
Turn these stones
into bread
You fool, I replied
they *are* bread

Forty days and
forty nights
I saw him each night
each morning
in many guises:
he came once as
Joseph
There is no death, said Satan
Oh yes there is, I said
get the hell
behind me

18 | On a high place
on a lonely tower
he showed me
the nations of the earth
and all to come
republics and empires
coronations and armies
public opinion polls
I wept

In the desert the night
is long and lonely
the thirty-seventh night
hallucinations of the Orient
opium
the thirty-eighth night
delusions of the western ocean
power
the thirty-ninth night

and the last
temptation:
to do nothing at all
to be human
to be language, not the Word
and to rest
in my father's arms
at last
the fortieth night

I woke

the forty-first dawn

I am standing on the shore of Galilee
a crew of fishermen are frying
their morning catch
They share it with me
It tastes so good
I laugh at their jokes

Listen, I say to them after a while
let me tell you all
about my dreams

Simon the fisherman
with his big clumsy hands, precise
only when mending his nets:
all the women of the shore in love with him,
and he with his head in the clouds
of Galilee:

Andrew his brother, but quite unlike him,
small, dark, a born sailor, with eyes
that could see a storm coming
an hour away across the lake:

I wanted them. I wanted them to be my friends,
companions on the dusty road, at times
bodyguards: and round the campfire at night
a simple human presence against the dark
that bore already the name of Golgotha.

I needed them. They were my supplements.
All of my teaching came down to this: God
can't do it alone, He needs more people.
He needs our help. The disciples
would fill the gap of my coming absence
and in turn seek others, against their death,
the chain continuing . . .

So Andrew became a sailor at last
and sailed the wine-dark sea
and came to the sun-stroked shore at Patras:
he stretched out arms and legs,
he welcomed his death, he sent his bones
sailing to Scotland.
He became the colour blue.

And Simon became Peter
the Rock
and on him I built the crazy
ramshackle rambling construction,
that architectural folly,
my Church.

I seldom saw my own face:
there were no mirrors
in the carpenter's workshop, there never
was glass for me to break.

Sometimes, over the side
of a fishing boat on Galilee,
I would see in still water some
reflection of God's grace.

Sometimes in a cup of wine
in the moment before I drank it down,
an image flickered on the surface.
This is my blood, I thought.

And later on I saw my face
as clear as a mirage of mountains
in every cripple, every beggar,
every blind eye raised to mine.

And later on I saw my face
as clear as a spirit level glass
in the face I chose to be my twin,
my life's companion:

mirror of my calmest water
blood of my darkest wine
Judas
Iscariot

What there will be at the end, I know,
is pain. Simply that: to be in the hands
of the torturer, the executioner,
all their exact knowledge
of what can be done to human bodies.

The body will scream.
The body, knowing this, screams already.
Do you think there is a day
that passes me in simple sunshine
without this foreknowledge?

Let this cup pass.
Let this cup pass from me.

I wash my hands after a meal
in the common bowl and watch
the water run red. Stigmata
before the fact. The wound in my side
opens every night, and like Thomas to come
I put my own hand into it,
doubting.

The problem with miracles is knowing
when to stop. Feed one multitude
and a thousand beggars start lining up;
cure one cripple and you might as well
open a clinic. And after Lazarus
every death was on my conscience.

I knew the arguments: God
may be omnipotent, but what He wants
is faith, not forced obedience.
A nice moral scruple, some might think,
in the face of famine. But what
was the alternative? For me

the miracles were merely tactics, a kind
of attention-getting device, I never
believed in them much myself.
I always saw the blind man
who couldn't see me. I turned away
each time more bitter, longing

for the simple pleasure of Cana,
attending the wedding feast and watching
the bride and the bridegroom dance together
in their white robes, with long-lashed eyes
smiling into each other, laughing like water
turned into wine.

Loaves and fishes —
basic, an approved diet —
I gave the multitude.

Five thousand on that hillside
the long afternoon, not knowing
how long I was to speak to them,
how long they had to stay.

Loaves of bread, the ritual
that will come to be spoken
by multitudes to come
in my name. In my flesh.
Taking the bread in my hands
I broke it, saying:
Take, eat, this is my body.
Loaves of bread.

And my name will be broken also,
broken like bread, acrostic
the name of the Fish:

   Ιησυζ Jesus
   Χριστοζ Christ
   Θεου   God's Ιχφυζ ⊶
   Υιοζ   Son
   Σωτηρ Saviour

I am the Gift, given.
I am all that there is

multiplied, disseminated
spread across that hillside
feeding the multitudes

torn apart.

Whose name, then, to give
in the single collapsed
moment of prayer? whose name
to address myself to?

In prayer we make ourselves one
with the Other; for me
there was no "Other." I am
all that there is, and all
there is to give. In the flesh
I am given. God —

shall I call you "father," male,
limiting myself
to half of my humanity?
Shall I call you "You"?

I could be just a voice in the wind,
a cry across the clifftop.
I could talk to myself like a hermit
too long in the desert.
I could pray: Father,
Father forgive me . . .

or retreat into silence
into the space
without any names, without any
longing —

is this prayer,
to wait
in that silence beyond naming
on the other
side of the tongue's
repeated desire?

This is my prayer:
to be, not the message,
but the envelope
of grace.

It's a cold night and the ground is hard.
Each way I turn, it seems an edge
of rock is nudging in my back. Today
I preached to a crowd of several hundred, healed
a leper and a cripple, but tonight
we're out in the wild, on the hills, and no one
has offered us a bed. I talked some more
with Peter, James and John, with Matthew;
and I felt the silence of Judas
hard at the edge of the group, like this stone
that keeps me awake. A normal day
on the road: small things accomplished,
a few seeds sewn. But I wish I could sleep,
I wish I could wish my own way
into dreams. I wish the stars were not
so cold above me, so precise in their patterns,
so eerily familiar, like a face
I know I have seen before, somewhere
I forget. The vigil of this night will be
the prayer I send to my father:
Father, I pray, father — forget me.
And thinking these words, in sudden awe
I fall asleep.

The stories I told
were simple stories: "a certain man,"
I said, and already
the audience was hooked.

I gave no details, no descriptions
of how they looked or
what they wore:
my listeners wrote the story
along with me
as we went.

Went, for instance, on the road
from Jerusalem down to Jericho:
a traveller got robbed,
they knew that road.
They knew its dangers.

A man with two sons, predictably
the one who stayed home and
the one who went bad.

No complicated plot twists: at the most
an unexpected moral in the end:
the prodigal forgiven, the good guy
turning out to be the Samaritan.

I loved these stories, their clear
and elegant lines, their narrative
minimalism —

but sometimes at night, before I slept,
these stories would grow and grow
like a pile of wood shavings
on a carpenter's floor: I followed them
down twisting roads that went
far beyond Jericho:

they became vast novels that would wait
centuries
before they could be written.
Those were the nights the traveller
died, abandoned, on the road;
the certain man became uncertain;
the prodigal came home and the elder brother
drove him away.

Those were the stories that fell
like seed onto stony ground.
None of them had happy endings.

Walking on water is
no trick: all you do
is step over the edge
and not look down.

Peter, I said, keep your
eyes on me: take one
step at a time: it's
easy. When he began

to sink, I hauled him
out of the waves and held him
dripping in my arms:
held him just as Joseph

had once held me (I was
learning to swim and
sinking into the water
every time he let me go).

In the quiet mauve of Capernaum twilight
the rich man came and spoke with me.
What must I do? he asked. Nicodemus —
you must be born again.

Understand me: I meant it literally.
I remember my birth.
I remember it as pain and light,
as compression of air
opening my lungs to cry:
the Word made Flesh. I remember
how much it hurt my mother.

You must be born again, I told him.
You must dance in the rhythm of the womb,
you must lie in the arms of God
and take milk from Her breast.

Nicodemus did not believe me.
He thought I was talking in riddles.

We sat on a rooftop in darkening light.
Consider the stars, I told him:
forever they are born, and born again
in total implosions of light.
They are as distant from us as you
will be from yourself. Your name
will be forgotten, or will reach you,
if it reaches you at all,
like light from a long-dead star.
To know your true name, Nicodemus,
you must be born again.

34 | All this he knew already:
had known it before he climbed the stair.
His eyes avoided mine, and all his breath
was leaving his body behind
like an embarrassed guest.

Transfiguration: the word
for when I truly became
light, and the image of light.

On the top of the mountain
with only three
of the twelve to witness

the perfect sign
not shown to the world:
pure presence, the trance

figuring all, all,
with no remainder. Afterwards
I lay exhausted,

my body shaking
as if in fever: the light
draining like water out of me.

Three of the twelve: Peter
and James and John —
I set them to guard

and slept for eleven hours.

Once it started,
the time of my preaching, the weeks
and months on the road, my wandering
all over Galilee, in circles
that looped to the south, ever closer
to Jerusalem —

once it started, there seldom was time
to be alone, or to return
to Nazareth, to the carpenter's shop
where my father's tools
gathered dust in each slow twilight —

there seldom was time.
But there were evenings when I came
and sat with my mother, watching
the shadows that never left her face
as she told me again

the story of the angel
the story of the years

she spent watching me grow, waiting
and waiting for the moment
when I too would turn towards her
my face
blazing in terrible fire
the face of the angel
with words of stone
and a sword of light
to strike into her heart

once it started

Lilies, I said, consider them —
I was aching with the beauty of the world
already no one had noticed —

lilies, I said, to a field of workers
had come to see me, their arms and backs
aching from long hours bent at the loom,

they toil not, I said, and neither
do they spin, they didn't notice, they wanted
to get home for a rest, for a wash —

and yet, I said, I say unto you
and they listened — why? — what was I
saying that could hold their attention,

they didn't want to hear about lilies
or to be told their toil was worthless, and I
didn't want to say that either, but I had to

tell them about the lilies, Solomon
I said, Solomon in all his glory
and each of them in their minds

remembered the finest cloth they'd ever spun,
regal, and decked it out with gold
and ornaments their eyes had never seen —

was not arrayed, I said, was not
arrayed like one of these
lilies — and my hand

dropped to the field we were standing in
where they hadn't noticed, they saw it now
for the first time, a field of lilies

and they shifted their feet uncomfortably
to see what they'd been trampling on,
Solomon in all his glory.

And I left it there, I said no more,
but I knew from a shiver in the wind
that all God's angels had gathered around me then

to consider the lilies.

I am the Light of the World,
I said. It was a metaphor.

The light flickers, a thin candle
in the great darkness. Imagine
a realm beyond language: that was
what I had to forget in the long
passage of my birth out of darkness
and into the light.

There is the woman who follows me,
Magdalene; she carries the light
inside her, in her eyes, I have seen it
shine there. This is, if you like,
a metaphor.

Sometimes I feel as if
I can *hear* the light: that thin,
that high mercury sound
that shimmers in the air like
sunlight on water. This is not
a metaphor: no, this is joy.

I am all the lights of the world:
but every minute a hand reaches out
somewhere to turn me off:
I flicker in this darkness, in the dim
lights of the word.

40 | But I know this now — when light
moved on the waves on the first
day of creation

that was me.

Lazarus, oh Lazarus —
the witnesses remember
that I wept.

Open the tomb, I told them —
and went down
into the smell of death.

You were waiting for me.
You knew I'd come, your
eyes were open.

I sat down beside you
there in the darkness;
you put your arm around me,

your dead arm,
to console me. To forgive me.
And I wept.

I take this coin
stamped in the image of Caesar,
a Roman nose on a
Roman face.

This is power;
this is the image of power.
A face in profile, encircled,
cut off at the neck.
Rub it between your fingers:
the face will fade,
but it will take time.

This is power; collect
enough of these coins, they become
an army of occupation.
They sit in your pockets like conquerors;
they demand a tribute
in kind. In coin.

I take this coin and toss it
into the air. Heads or tails?
If I wanted to make a miracle,
it need never come down.

Render unto Caesar
the things
that are
Caesar's.

Centurion, he marches towards me
as if at the head of his legions: my hands
clench into fists, feeling the pain
of nails driven into my bones. Roman,
he stands before me with all his power

abandoned — he falls to his knees
(heavy in clumsy armour), he tries
and fails to speak, he gasps
"My daughter," and he is only

a man, over whose head
my hands unclench in blessing
(though still the imprint of nails
is traced, stigmata, on my palms).

Meanwhile his daughter waits for me:
a life to be redeemed, another
job to be done. My voice in the silence
whispers to her death: "Arise."

The death by small stones —

not jagged rocks to crush
the forehead in the first
merciful minute

but the small smooth stones
separate, accumulating, so
the punishment is knowledge
how long it will last —

that's what they decided.
Those men.
Those givers of law.
While she

who had loved the wrong one,
who had been taken
out of his bed, out of the reach
of his arms to protect her,
she —

taken in the act
I knew of but had never known —

she was crouched at my feet, she was
clutching my robe, her hands
performing an embrace —

and I heard my own voice
as if from a distance, saying
"Let he among you
who is without sin
cast the first stone . . ."

knowing the only one there
who was without sin
was me —

one hand resting on her head
and one hand holding a small smooth stone.

46| Another night denied
the comfort of sleep; grey dawn
beginning to lighten the lake,
cold mist
seeping out of the ground
like breath. Last night
I stumbled against an edge of rock, I
cut my knee open, it
hurts . . .

(When I was a child, I could run
always to my mother in the faith
she would make it all better
— as mothers do, while the blood
spills through their fingers.)

. . . it hurts, and I have no one.
I have left my mother long behind,
though I feel her with me every day
when I reach out my hands
to the blind, to the lame, when I
make it all better,
even the lepers. Mary is there,

Mary is with me. So last night
I did not wish for any miracle
to close my own wound: I wanted her
to come and heal me, hold me
with her hair surrounding my face
as if again it could be Nazareth
and I be five years old.

Listen, this is all I have
to tell you: that love
and power are one. Is it
really that simple? I promise you,
it is.

Why else should I have come here?
What sense would it make
if I did not die?

Listen to my heart
as the sun comes up over Galilee
— do you think I do not love this world?
Do you think that flesh and bone
were ever dearer to me? Listen

as I turn my face south
towards Jerusalem, towards
the holy city of my death:

all that I have to tell you
is here

            in this reluctance of my step
            in the stuttering song

                    of my terrified heart

Temptation does not cease: it is never
once and for all, a meeting on a mountain
that decides the issues, bang, like a lid
slammed on a jar of serpents. Satan
doesn't know the meaning of the word No:
he insinuates his questions, again, into even
your smallest satisfactions. Rather than cure
a cripple here or there, why not abolish death?
enforce by sudden miracle a peace
to end all wars? or proclaim
apocalypse now, the lifting of the veil
and truth, unhidden, manifest to all?
Why this messy inefficient way
through death, through pain, through a stubborn
need for belief? The ultimate tyrant,
God doesn't want to be obeyed, He wants
to be loved. The arrogant bastard.

Lucifer, Lucifer, Prince of the Morning,
how lucid the light of your logic!
How I long to believe you — believe me,
the palms of my hands are itching
with the longing to believe you. Liar,
lovely deceiver. My surrogate twin.

Is it enough, three years,
enough to lay the foundations
for the rest of history?

I observe how Matthew now
walks straight ahead, having lost
the sideways shuffle, the averted eye
of the tax collector. I see
how Peter strains to build his strength
upon the very flaws that split
the rock I named him after:
and how Andrew daily settles
into the deep sea of his silence.

Have they heard enough?
My words they will remember,
will forget. Will make up new ones,
as if to a song: no matter,
the tune will carry them.
But still they think within the bounds
of Galilee, Capernaum —
not even yet Jerusalem.
Whenever I turn south, they
grow uneasy. Is it enough,
three years?

And Judas by now must know
I am not the one he was waiting for.
I am not the Messiah of fire,
the warrior of holy slaughter.
The dome of the Temple is free
from the wrath of my hand.

I have cured some lepers; I have not
cured leprosy. What good then
have I done? he asks me.
I ask myself.

Judas by now must know
what it is he was born to do.

This is the text
proclaimed in prophecy:

Behold your King
riding, like a Fool, on a donkey
into the city he has come to claim,
into the city of the end of time.

I am the reading of this text,
I offer myself to your
interpretation.

Spread branches of palm
for me to ride on:
wave their great leaves in the air
till the wind
like a trumpet trembles.

I am what is written.
I am your Fool.
I am your King.

52 | God damn the buyers and
sellers of God! God curse
their tables and trades, their
baubles and souvenirs: as if
God's grace were groceries,
doves for a bargain price
and your soul on a sliding scale
at a special discount! God
in God's house, *my* house, mocked
and marred by the market,
marked-down greed. My curse
and my hand upon them: overturn
these tables, give me a scourge
and I'll drive them out like
scavenging dogs onto the mean
streets of Jerusalem!

> (My house, I said — and behind
> their beards they took note,
> a word in the High Priest's ear:
> blasphemed. Blasphemed.)

Behind me the wreckage of their commerce,
tables in splinters, cashboxes scattered.
I'm standing there breathless, the anger
dying out of my eyes like an evening prayer.
A dozen underfed doves
go fluttering to freedom
in the sky.

Jerusalem from the Mount of Olives —
my beloved city, how brief
the time I have spent within your walls!

First light of morning
pale on the silver screen of olive leaves
flickers its shadows, like a flight of birds,
over each wall of bleached-out clay:
uncertain time of margin, not yet day
and the night just slipping sideways past
like a reluctant lover, committing
one final kiss on the threshold
of a secret room —

so I have loved you, Jerusalem, and so
I weep for you now, foreknowing
all your long history, seeing
the Temple Mount divided by barbed wire —

this morning of Passover,
the bakeries in every alley filling
the air with the smell
of unleavened bread —

my heart is breaking for your beauty, oh
Jerusalem, Jerusalem.

54| This is my body
broken for you

These are my words
broken for you

my words made flesh
become writing

torn, scraps in the wind
my body on a dusty road

I give unto you
my body, which is bread

take me in your mouth, consume me
this is my body inside yours

broken by the hammer
pierced by the nails

Do this again and again
in remembrance of me

And then take this —
this is my blood

In the garden

I entered the hourglass of time,
the moment when all my life of prayer
reduced to a single cry:
if it is possible, *if*
there is any other way —
oh Father take
take this cup from my lips
I prayed
— while even on that hard cold ground
my best friends slept

In the garden

I offered my cheek to his kiss,
Judas, with thirty pieces of silver
jangling in his throat
and my hand in the cool of his hair
gave him the blessing
he had worked so hard to gain

In the garden

what I find I remember most clearly
is that dash of colour, brilliant crimson
stump of the soldier's ear, his
wild indignity at being wounded so, and then
the dumb amazement, disbelief
when I touched it, fast, with my fingers

before they lead me away, and left him
healed again, uncertain (except for the blood
that stained the shoulder of his tunic) whether
any of this
had really happened.

At last I know (King Fool)
what the body is made of.
The human body. It is made of pain.

Crown of thorns: each point
gashes the blood from my temple
till it runs into the corners of my mouth —
thirsty, I drink myself in
like vinegar.

What is truth? asks Pilate —
my back flayed open by his whips,
and still he has to ask.

The soldier lines up the nail,
blunt point to the palm of my hand:
lifts the hammer awkwardly
above his head — you're
holding it wrong, I want to tell him,
some carpenter you are, you'll
hurt your back, here
let me show you —

        but then the pain
        at last takes over.

58 | A thief is hung on either side, a certain
symmetry.
One of them curses me; one of them prays —
prays that I will remember
even in this final hour. Yet I have stolen
more than they did: I have taken their time
as I will take yours — I will come
like a thief in the night, to snatch again
the joy of being human, of being alive
even in this final hour. Let me bless
them both: the one who puts his trust in memory,
the other in forgetting: not just
the story's repentant sinner but also
this man who meets death cursing,
his dying screams of pain and anger
refusing to be comforted. Today,
today I tell you both, today you will be
with me in Paradise. And there
we shall all be thieves together.

I am the Light of the World
going dim, going out.
Darkness at noon,
the day goes blind,
something weighs on my chest,
choking me, I haul myself
up by the pain
in my hands and feet, I
rest and breathe on the
iron of the nails, I
cannot see clearly, is
my mother with me
watching my death?
Mother, listen, the angel
is here again and speaking to you:
blessed be
the fruit of your womb, most
fortunate among women — mother
do you see the angel,
see his eyes? and then
do you see mine, still,
are they still open,
mother,
can you still see my eyes?

Smoothing one last splinter with a sweep of his plane,
Joseph regards the work he has done, the day's
good labour completed. He sets down his tools
and lights the lantern that hangs by the door.
I am playing on the floor with a shaving of wood,
I am five years old. He hoists me to his shoulder
and together we turn to the door. Outside

the day is growing dark, there is
a trembling in the earth, a thunder
as heaven itself splits open, the Veil
of the Temple tears apart — Father,

into your hands I commend my spirit.

On the threshold Joseph pauses, one last time
looks back at what he has made, and smiles.

Strange moment in the tomb
my eyes flick open, try
to adjust to the darkness —

like waking from a dream, you
don't yet know where you are, then
placing myself again

inside this body, inside
its memory of wounds: my hands
pierced and unhealed, but pain

is no longer a part, it seems,
of this new kind of
being alive. Being alive in the world

walking on grass in the freshness of dew,
the scent of olive trees in the morning
sunlight where the women see me —

oh Lord, oh Father, it is all
so beautiful.
I am home again.

62 | Thomas, come here, this is the moment we've
both been waiting for, always already
signed in your name: Thomas: to doubt
and then to put your fingers on the truth

inside the body. As if you were reading braille
you can enter my wounds: you can feel the broken
small bones of the palm where the nail
smashed through. You can thrust your left hand

deep into my side: is it warm in there?
Can you scan the metres of my blood
and tell the stories of my halting breath?
Inside the body, where the last truth lies.

So why draw back now, Thomas? why
prefer the abstract profession of faith
when I offer this chance no man will have again:
to get to the heart of matter, to erase

all signatures of doubt inside the bones of God?

On the road to Emmaus
it is as if I am here
and not here, both at once, my feet

stepping firm on the dusty ground,
and my throat, dry like yours,
thirsting for wine. And yet

at times I disappear,
I swim at the edges of your vision,
you think I am a ghost, I am

not a ghost. I am here
and not here, both at once, I am
with you always, like this

on the road to Emmaus.

> (You know you will never
> get to Emmaus. It is not a place
> that anyone arrives at, only
>
> a destination, somewhere ahead,
> an idea you can aim for
> when you walk with me.)

64 | Surely when I ascended
it was into Grace

Last morning I am with you,
a slight breeze blowing
over the mountaintop: my friends
I am leaving behind,
who will walk from this place
on tufts of grass, on dusty paths,
on the solid earth —

while I once more
am dissolved into Light,
am become again
not words but The Word

cast out from any language, unspoken
but speaking always,
speaking my loss, my regret, my desire

for tufts of grass, for dusty paths

for a group of women and men
friends of mine

who walk down a hill at lunchtime

into grace

When I come back
it will be as a carpenter.

HEATHER SPEARS

About the Author

In 1980, Stephen Scobie won the
Governor General's Award for *McAl-
mon's Chinese Opera.* In 1989, he was
shortlisted for the Governor Gener-
al's Award for *Dunino.* Stephen Sco-
bie's long and productive career has
taken him from Scotland, where he
was born, to the Canadian prairies
and then to Vancouver Island where
he teaches at the University of Vic-
toria. He has been a co-chairperson
of the League of Canadian Poets, a
member of the experimental sound
poetry performance group Re:Sound-
ing, a member of many journals' edi-
torial boards, a founding editor of
Longspoon Press, and the author of
an extensive list of books, including
Remains and *Alias Bob Dylan,* both
published by Red Deer College Press.

THE WRITING WEST POETRY SERIES
FROM RED DEER COLLEGE PRESS